# A-Z of

# Animal Poems

# 2

P.D. Cain

ISBN-13: 978-1511907774

This is the 2nd A to Z of Animals poems book. Both are animal picture books and introduce children to poetry and rhyme. Animal books for kids you could say, although adults will find them fun to read as well.

Discover other titles by P.D. Cain (Captain Peter):-

Percy the Parrot and other pet subjects
Percy the Parrot 2 – the bird's perspective

A Sign of the Rhymes

A-Z of Animal Poems

Visit Captain Peter's website for up to date information:-

**www.captainpeter.net**.

Meercats, Nip and Tuck, they are quite a pair,
They do everything together, go everywhere.
But, what has stopped them in their tracks?
What has made them stop and stare?
Or, are they just on lookout, to guard against
attacks,
From something that is out there, perhaps?
If you want to see what they see,
Then why not take a look,
At the animal poems from A to Zee,
which are contained within this book.

# CONTENTS

## CLIVE THE ANTELOPE

Clive the antelope had very springy feet,
When he sensed danger, he could make a speedy
retreat,

He was so fast; he could not be beaten,
Which meant he wasn't likely to be eaten,

Some predators regularly tried to catch Clive,
But his speed and agility kept him alive.

## BUZZ THE BEE

*I am Buzz the bee,*
*I help to make honey,*
*I am a worker bee you see,*
*And I am not lazy.*

*There are bees that sit around and moan,*
*Who do nothing but stay at home,*
*These lazy bees are called drones.*

*These drones do nothing and only skive,*
*But sometime soon the day will arrive,*
*When these laziest of bees will get thrown out of*
*the hive,*
*Then I'd like to see how they stay alive.*

*I will just continue to be hard working,*
*You will never find me shirking,*
*So around the flowers you may see me,*
*My name is Buzz and I am a bee.*

# CARMEL THE CAMEL

Carmel the Camel, she had the hump,
Not so much a hump really, but more like a stump.
"Why can't I be like other camels?" she thought with dismay,
"Why was her body looking so horribly this way?"

She dreamed wistfully for a real proper hump,
One that would be prominent,
Two humps, even better, they would be brilliant.

She'd heard of a camel, who, in camel folklore, was legendary,
He had three humps on his back and his name was Humphrey,
Carmel thought though, that three humps was too much,
And would probably make her look a bit big and butch.

Then Carmel came back to earth with a bump,
And realised she would only ever have one hump,
She needed to work on the stump that she had,
And if it would just grow that bit bigger, it
wouldn't be so bad.

She would work on her stump's size by chewing
the fat,
Now that she'd got over her brief little spat,
Eventually her stump size would grow bigger and
firm.
Patience is a virtue is what she had to learn.

# CHARLIE THE CHIMPANZEE

Charlie, who was a chimpanzee,
Liked to swing from tree to tree,
He was a cheeky little monkey.

Charlie hung out with a gang of pals,
Trying to show off in front of the gals,
When together, they had no morals.

They were quite rude and had no poise,
Laughed a lot and made loads of noise,
Charlie liked being one of the boys.

But when on his own, he could be friendly,
Being funny and almost saintly.
Yes Charlie was a cheeky little monkey.

## JAKE THE DOG

*I know a dog called Jake,*
*Many friends he would like to make,*
*But because he is fierce and mean,*
*His softer side is rarely seen,*
*And his barking keeps people awake.*

*He tries and tries to show that he's good,*
*But people think he's after their blood,*
*They won't go near him; they think he's vicious,*
*Because his breed are considered as dangerous*
*So Jake, poor thing, is misunderstood.*

*He knows there are others just like him,*
*Who are genuinely not nice and like bitin',*
*Their owners train them to be aggressive,*
*And some of the dogs become hyperactive,*
*Worse still, some are used for fightin'*

But Jake himself is not really that bad,
But he's tarred with the same brush, which is sad.
His shouts for attention go unheeded,
It's just not fair in how he is treated,
People see Jake and think he's just barking mad.

## DOLLY THE DOLPHIN

Dolly the dolphin likes to swim,
In the great big ocean she lives in.
She loves to play in waves that are rough,
She plays and plays until she's had enough,
Dolly the dolphin is made of tough stuff.

She's found a mate to share her fun,
And they keep playing until they're done,
So she's glad that she is not the only one,
And now they've started courtin'

# ERIC THE EAGLE

Eric the eagle had eyes that could see for miles,
The only problem was, he wasn't very agile,
He would hover in the sky all day,
Until he saw some tasty prey,

He'd work out his tactics as he dived,
But his prey outmanoeuvred him as he arrived.
Occasionally Eric would be in luck,
But if you do see Eric, you'd better duck.

## FLO THE FLAMINGO

Flo was a flamingo, and she was tickled pink,
For she saw someone she fancied and he gave her
the wink.
With his alluring eyes he beckoned her to go and
dance with him,
His legs were long, his neck was sleek, he looked so
fit and trim.
Flo could not resist his manly charms once he
started dancin'.

Flo joined in the dance with him; she found it so
much fun,

*She decided that he was for her, the courtship had begun.*
*Before long they were joined together, as if like man and wife,*
*And went on to have many children and endured much trouble and strife,*
*But Flo always stood by her man and was with him for the rest of her life.*

# GORDON THE GOLDFISH

Gordon was a goldfish, who lived in a glass bowl,
He was all on his lonesome with no friends, poor
soul.

He'd swim around, and around, and around all
day long,
He thought he would sing to himself, but he didn't
know a song.

But fortunately a goldfish's memory lasts just a
few seconds,
So he didn't have to wait long before a new life
beckoned!

## HETTY THE HEDGEHOG

*Hetty the hedgehog, she once got quite prickly,*
*It wasn't that she was feeling hot, or that she was*
*feeling sickly.*
*Some indelicate soul told everyone she had fleas,*
*Which Hetty was aware of, but she was being*
*teased.*
*Hetty wasn't best pleased!*

*The fact that the fleas gave Hetty some little*
*thrills,*
*She loved it when they tickled her as they crept*
*between her quills,*

*But for someone to say horrible things about her,*

Did they not understand that the fleas gave her
pleasure?
However, Hetty was a fighter.

She discovered the perpetrator, who she faced
without fear,
It was Molly the mole, who was being so insincere,
Hetty shouted at her for all to hear
Reducing Molly the mole to tears.
Yes, Hetty gave her a right flea in the ear!

## ISABELA THE IBERIAN LYNX

*Isabela is an Iberian Lynx,*
*Whose species became almost extinct.*
*But now she is safe, she thinks.*

*There was a time she worried about her fate,*
*And dreamed of having children with a perfect*
*mate,*
*But how much longer did she have to wait?*

*Then some good people on the Iberian Peninsula,*
*Went about saving this lovely creature,*
*So on the Iberian Landscape they can again*
*feature.*

*In order for these people to succeed,*
*They had to find Isabela a male she fancied,*
*And then they could begin to breed.*

*They found her Liandro, who she thought divine,*
*And they went about saving the Iberian Lynx line,*
*Now it looks like they were saved just in time.*

*Through these people's hard work and dedication,*
*It is hoped that these animals' numbers will strengthen,*
*And have Isabela and Liandro contributing to their conservation.*

*For Isabela it seems perfectly clear,*
*That for now, she has nothing to fear,*
*But still, she is going to play it by ear.*

# ISIDRO THE IBEX

*Isidro the Ibex, he likes to act the goat,*
*Usually in places that are quite remote,*
*Playfully, he hops along the mountain tops,*
*Especially on rocks that have sheer drops.*
*He certainly is an animal of note.*

*It's not all fun and games as his life can be complex,*
*For Isidro occasionally locks horns with some other Ibex,*
*He maybe fighting for his honour, or fighting in play,*
*He has to show he's the master in every way,*
*But usually his fights are over the opposite sex.*

*Isidro likes it on his little mountain spot,*
*And defends his domain with everything he's got,*
*But most of the time he likes to act silly,*
*Because Isidro can be a right silly billy,*
*I reckon Isidro would make a good mascot!*

## INNES THE INDRI

Innes the Indri is strangely demure,
Especially for a Lemur.

She appears reclusive and somewhat shy,
Then she transfixes you with a staring eye.

She seems to be quiet and doesn't make a sound,
Then she opens her mouth and she's heard for
miles around.

*She finds a tree which she likes to sit on,*
*But in one quick leap, you'll find that she's gone.*

*Yes Innes the Indri would go quite far,*
*If she wasn't stuck in Madagascar.*

# JAZZ THE JAGUAR

Jazz, she is a Jaguar,
And she's been spotted by a talent spotter,
But what has this talent spotter spotted. Could he make her a star?
He was about to place Jazz on the spot after seeing her from afar.
For the talent spotter was called Jim and he himself was a Jaguar.

Jim had spotted that Jazz was sleek and in tip top condition,
And Jim was looking for a mate to knock spots off the competition.

Gently, gently towards the spot where Jazz lay asleep,
And once Jim reached a certain spot, he made a lover's leap,
But Jazz had acted clever; she had spotted what Jim was plotting,
She too was looking for a mate and it was her that was talent spotting.

And so Jazz and Jim got married on the spot,
Now they have lots of spotty little Jaguars,
It's quite a family they've got.

# KARRIE THE KANGAROO

Karrie the Kangaroo wished she was as light as a feather,
Now she had to think quick and had to box clever.
This was no time to sit and slouch,
She had her young daughter inside her pouch.

A pack of dingoes had her surrounded,
Her fears for their lives were very well founded.
She had to move quickly, before it was too late,
Her decision made now would decide their fate.

The dingoes howled loudly, they were a vicious bunch,
They wanted these kangaroos for today's lunch
But Karrie knew exactly what to do,
She was a very clever kangaroo.

With a spring in her step, she made one big bound,
And in no time at all she travelled fast over ground.
The dingoes gave chase, but it was to no avail,
Karrie outran them, those dingoes had failed.

# KENNY THE KEEL BILLED TOUCAN

*Kenny the Keel Billed Toucan from South America,*
*Always likes to give that little bit extra.*
*He is flamboyant and quite a colourful character,*
*He sticks his beak into things that don't matter.*

*He watches closely everyone's comings and goings,*
*Yes he sticks his nose into all sorts of things,*
*But his bright persona and his colourful wit,*
*Usually allows him to get away with it.*

*His main ambition he would like to fulfil,*
*Is to be king of the toucans and be top of the bill.*

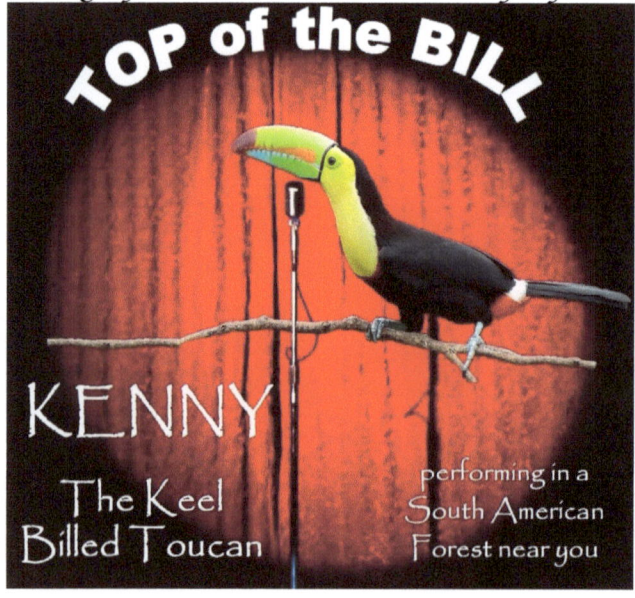

# LENA THE LLAMA

Lena was a Llama,
Who could make a crisis out of a drama,
She had a propensity to exaggerate,
Her own and everyone else's fate.

Lena and others lived on a farm,
Where everything would normally be calm,
But Lena always imagined the worst,
And said that they were all cursed.

One time when the farmer wanted to shear Llama
wool,
Lena convinced everyone that there was going to
be a cull,
To clear his farm of every Llama,
Lena caused lots of trouble for that poor farmer.

The farmer was kind and loved each animal,
And the shearing of wool was always annual.
Lena could cause trouble in an empty barn,
Always spinning a believable yarn.

Lena loved how everyone trusted what she said,
And knew how the other Llamas could be easily
led.

Then one day, Lena got her comeuppance,
When the farmer realised she was a nuisance,
He sold Lena to another farmer for a pittance.
As Lena left, they all said good riddance
Lena is no longer a hindrance,
For where she now lives, there are no Llamas present,
Lena now lives a lonely existence.

## MARLENE THE MANATEE

Marlene is a Manatee and you can see how,
A Manatee is commonly known as a sea cow.
She swims in shallow waters, where it's nice and warm,
And lives in the same area where she was born.

There was once a drunken sailor, in those waters he did wade,
And when he saw Marlene, he mistook her for a mermaid.
Marlene thought it amusing, the big mistake the sailor made,
But the look on that sailor's face is a memory she wouldn't trade.

# NORMAN THE NUMBAT

Norman is worried that he is getting fat,
This is not good for a little Numbat,
He's been gorging himself on the food he most likes,
Yes, Norman has been eating lots and lots of termites.

He had been feasting alongside his younger brother,
And both of them were told not to be greedy by there Numbat mother.
They had all come across a huge termite's nest,
And they tucked into it with a little too much zest.

Norman was suffering from his over-indulgence,
Perhaps in future, he will have more sense.
The next time he feels having greedy intentions,
He will eat those tasty termites in moderation.

# ERNIE THE OWL

*I am an owl and my name is Ernie,*
*Some people think of me as wise,*
*I observe my surroundings sternly,*
*With my large, all seeing eyes.*

*But beneath my serious persona,*
*I am really quite a hoot,*
*And although I appear a loner,*
*I'm not a miserable old coot.*

## SKEET THE POND SKATER

*I can walk on water, I can also fly,*
*But I prefer walking on water to flying, so I don't even try.*
*On the water I have much more fun,*
*On it I cannot only walk, but I can also run.*
*Well it is more of a hop really, but it is of no consequence,*
*What I can do on water, it really is immense.*

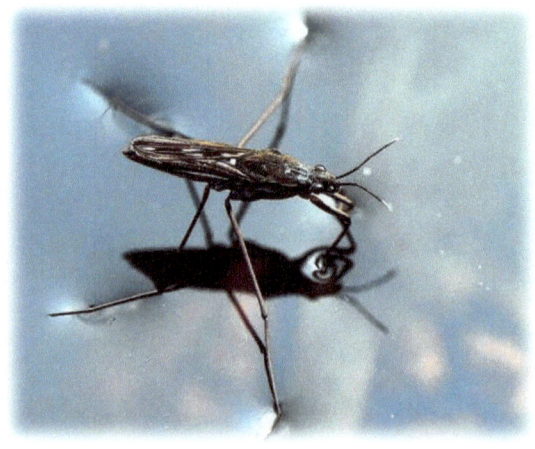

*My ability is down to my legs, which are long and hairy,*
*I also have a pair of wings, but I am not a fairy!*
*Some think, I am really swimming, but I am no faker.*
*My name is Skeet and I am a Pond Skater.*

## QUENTIN THE QUETZAL

*My name is Quentin and I am a Quetzal,*
*I am a bird that is very colourful.*
*I have bright coloured feathers of blue, red and green,*
*I am the most beautiful bird that you've ever seen.*
*My tail is long and sleek,*
*And I have a little yellow beak,*

*I'm from Central America where I live high in the trees,*
*But as you see from my plumage, I like to please.*

*I know I have a very pretty face,*
*I'm really too good for this place.*
*I'm a bit of a show off, somewhat over the top,*
*But I am who I am and I would not swap.*

## ROBIN THE RACCOON

Robin the Raccoon was a bit of a bandit,
He was very clever and was not a dimwit.

He would enter the house with his black mask on,
Steal something fast, and then he was gone.

Robbing was his favourite game,
But beneath his thick fur, he was really quite
tame.

Robin, to me, is not any sort of threat,
Because this Raccoon is my little pet.

## SCOTT THE SCORPION

*Scott, the Scorpion has a sting in his tail,*
*It doesn't half hurt and you won't half wail.*
*His cousins are worse, for their sting can be deadly,*
*Even so, never get Scott even remotely angry.*
*He's a bad tempered so and so, like the rest of his family,*
*None of them are very nice and are usually quite nasty.*

# SANDRA THE SEAHORSE

Sandra the Seahorse had been taken for a ride,
And it was all because someone had lied.
She was asked for a favour by her best mate Sue,
Which Sandra was only too willing to do.
Now she's saddled with a problem, it's really unfair,
It's all turned into a horrible nightmare.

It all started when Sue asked Sandra to go on a date,
She said it was just an old school mate,
But when Sandra turned up at the arranged time and place,
She realised this date had a familiar face.
It was Sue's boyfriend, his name was Rod,
The whole situation seemed a bit odd.

Rod looked bemused when Sandra arrived,
Both wondered what it was that Sue had contrived.
After a brief chat, they decided 'Whatever',
And so went out for the evening together.

During the evening Rod was increasingly imposing,
And began to call Sandra his little darling.
Sandra was flattered by Rod's attention and

many kind words,
*And by the end of the night, they were like a pair
of lovebirds.*

*Rod exclaimed that his relationship with Sue was
going to end.*
*Sandra felt guilty. She had betrayed her friend.*
*It turned out that this is what Sue had planned,*
*But why? Sandra didn't understand.*

*Sandra thought that Rod was a handsome and
strong Seahorse,*
*But it was soon apparent as love took it's course.*
*She found that Rod was extremely possessive,*
*And could at times be very aggressive.*

*Sandra was unable to move without Rod being
there,*
*The situation had become a real nightmare.*
*She'd trusted her friend Sue. She got her into this
mess.*
*Rod was causing Sandra so much stress.*

Sandra had to find a way out of her situation,
She could not live with all this tension.
She'd had enough and so one day,
She packed her bags and ran away.
She moved to a place where she could safely hide,
Determined to never again be taken for a ride.

## TARQUIN THE TARSIER

*Tarquin the Tarsier has been told that he must get a grip,*
*He needs to let go of that tree he clings to and form a courtship.*
*There's a nice female Tarsier who's been making big eyes at him,*
*But he'd better be quick in making a move, before he's left out on a limb.*

*If he could just get a spring in his step, he'd be with her like a shot,*
*And after a brief romance they could maybe tie the knot.*
*All it needs is for Tarquin to make the first move,*
*But his eyes are heavier than his brain is and thinks he has nothing to prove.*

*What are we to do with him? What enthusiasm can we inject?*
*Perhaps that female Tarsier could coax him over with a nice tasty insect.*

# URSULA THE URCHIN

Ursula was an urchin with a bubbly character,
She was the shape of a ball, but not everyone liked
her,
She was sometimes subjected to abuse and scorn,
And wished she hadn't such a well rounded form,

But Ursula was a proud urchin with an honour to
protect,
And as her spines were very sharp, she used them
to good effect.

One time some little urchin needled Ursula about
her size,

*So she pinned the offender to a rock and made him apologise,*

*Still, Ursula dreamed that somewhere out there in the deep ocean,*
*Is some handsome urchin to lavish her with love and devotion.*

# VLADIMIR THE VAMPIRE BAT

*Vladimir the Vampire Bat is really spitting blood,*
*He was told to leave his home and he doesn't see*
*why he should.*
*It wasn't him that went off and a had a little*
*flutter,*
*But he was accused of being at fault. Did they*
*think he was a sucker?*

*It was his missus, who had a gambling habit, the*
*horses she liked best,*
*But she wasn't very lucky and she lost everything*
*they possessed.*

*Now Vladimir's blood was boiling, he had to
protect them from eviction,*
*He also had to think about how he could stop his
wife's addiction*

*It was not as if it was blood money that Vladimir
had to pay,*
*Perhaps a loan from a bank would keep the
creditors at bay.*
*He needed to organise something quick, but it was
like getting blood from a stone,*
*But Vladimir needed to protect his assets, and
hopefully keep his home.*

*Vladimir also had a family; he had to protect his
flesh and blood,*
*He felt quite optimistic that they would come out
of it for the good.*
*He decided to be more firm with his wife, amongst
other things.*
*"She won't get any money from me" he thought, "I
will hold the purse strings"*

*He'd been given a bloody nose; he'd almost gone
insane,*
*He didn't care if there was some bad blood. It
wasn't going to happen again.*

# JACK THE VIETNAMESE POTBELLIED PIG

My name is Jack and I am a Vietnamese
Potbellied Pig,
My hair is black and I like to dig.
I use my snout to dig up the ground,
I also do other things when no-one is around.

You see, I am kept in a pig pen, which I think is
wrong,
You may think I'm small, but I am very very
strong.
I like to use my strength to uproot my pen's
fencing,
Which keeps being rebuilt, but I am unrelenting,

I also have to live with some clucking hens,
Who fortunately live in their own pens,
They can be noisy and send me round the bend,
So I dig up their fence too and let them into the
gardens.

*My owners don't understand why I keep escaping,*
*They suspect it is me, and I hear them complaining,*
*But I like my freedom and I'll continue to dig,*
*After all, I am a Vietnamese Potbellied Pig.*

## WALLY THE WALRUS

*Wally the Walrus is a bit long in the tooth,*
*He doesn't like telling lies, he just states the truth.*
*He can't be doing with these young bucks,*
*Who try and trick him and chance their luck,*
*Attempting to take over Wally's 'Harem',*
*Which he defends vigorously to the very extreme.*

*Wally's been around for a long time now,*
*And he knows intimately each one of his cows.*
*Wally exerts himself fiercely, lest those youngsters forget,*
*That there's still plenty of life in this old Walrus yet.*

# WANDA THE WOODPECKER

Wanda the Woodpecker had a big headache,
It was so bad, it was more than she could take.

Her friend advised her about a new type of therapy,
Which varied in both strength and intensity,
Wanda decided to take the strongest dose,
This resulted in her becoming somewhat morose,

One particular pole was doing her head in,
Her beak, and her head, were really achin'
Then someone suggested she make a hole,
In some wooden tree - and not a concrete pole!
Wanda felt a little foolish, but she kept her pecker up,
After all, it was just a tiny hiccup.

# XANTI THE XANTUS'S MULLERET

Xanti the Xantus's Mulleret, told her boyfriend to go and whistle,
So he flew off thinking she was being fickle.
Off he went flying over the ocean,
Leaving behind Xanti and her abnormal emotion.

She began to feel bad - and lonely too,
So she put her pride aside and off she flew.

They were an item, they were a pair,
Their adventures at sea they liked to share.
When hunting for fish they dived in together.
From which they derived so much pleasure.

So when Xanti caught up with her boyfriend,
Her apologies to him she did extend.
"Please forgive me" she had to beg,
"I'm about to lay our first egg".

*Her boyfriend Xap was thrilled and delighted*
*And both of them became very excited.*
*So off they went diving into the sea,*
*For soon they will be a family of three.*

# XENOS THE XENOP

Xenos the Xenop can be a bit of a creep,
For you can't really see him, until he cheeps,
His colour is the same as the wood on the trees,
So he's harder to find than other birdies.

He seems to be a mystery to some,
But he's not in any way a villain,
He acts a bit like an old woman,
Making his nest look like a clay oven.

Xenos is aware of people that are looking,
But he knows exactly as to what's cooking,
Their eyes may be pointed in his direction,
So he just stays still to avoid detection,

Xenos the Xenop lives down in Mexico,
And even down into South America you know,

But if you want to find him, he could make you weep,
For being well concealed is how he likes to keep.

# YIPI THE YETI

There was a yeti called Yipi,
Who looked a bit like a hippy,
In the cold night air,
His long shaggy hair,
Stopped him from getting too nippy.

Some people didn't believe he existed,
And to come out to disprove them, he resisted,
He kept himself hidden within the Himalayan white snow,
Leaving only big foot imprints for people to follow,
Remaining unfound, as an animal, he's not listed.

# EWOK THE YORKIE

*I maybe small, but I'm neither bald nor porky,*
*I have lovely hair and I am a Yorkie.*
*Yorkshire terrier that is and my name is Ewok,*
*It's a name from Star Wars, so I'm no Mister*
*Spock!*

*I am friendly, loyal, and brave; Oh and I love to*
*walk,*
*The only thing I cannot do is speak human talk.*
*You can take me anywhere; you can rely on me,*
*I seldom get upset, or get angry.*
*I will be your friend, for ever and ever,*
*Because I am Ewok, a Yorkshire terrier.*

*I also have a friend called Daisy,*
*She is a sort of relation,*
*Now you may think that this sounds crazy,*
*But she works for a radio station,*

She has the job as their mascot,
Looking pretty in her pink dress,
Many friends that Daisy has got,
And she's their 'little princess'.

She is really friendly to everyone,
Except if you try and brush her hair,
Then you'll get a fierce reaction,
And her teeth she will then bear.

There is only one that has permission,
Only one that has the right,
To brush Daisy's hair without confliction,
For this princess is in love with a knight.

## ZENA THE ZEBU

Zena was a Zebu, and she was a little cow,
Because she was only small, it gave her a complex
somehow.
There were bigger cows than her, of which she was
well aware,
And her only being four feet tall, didn't seem very
fair.

Many times Zena would be teased, which gave her
an attitude,
And when it got too upsetting, she just moo'd and
moo'd.
This spurred on those bigger cows, to tease her
even more,

Zena was an object of ridicule, which was difficult to ignore.

Zena had to find a way to stop those big cow bullies,
She began to look at her antagonists as a bunch of dummies.
She turned on her abusers; she showed them that she was tough,
She was unrelenting in what she did, until they'd had enough.

Zena happened to be clever with words, those big cows lacked intelligence,
She now shows them who is boss, they in turn show her reverence,
Zena proved that being small does not have to be debilitating,
And that taking charge of ones own life proved quite stimulating.

# ABOUT THE AUTHOR

P.D. Cain (Captain Peter) is an Englishman, originally from the Peak District in Derbyshire, England, and now lives on the Algarve in Portugal. He is know as 'Captain Peter' because he provides a 'Seawatch Report' for Kiss Fm Portugal, and has done for over fifteen years. He also skippers tourist boats during the summer season.

He has written a number of books:-
A-Z of animal Poems (1 & 2)
A Sign of the Rhymes

Percy the Parrot – and other pet subjects
Percy the Parrot – the bird's perspective
April Dawn – *Life Lives*

Also, a number of non-fiction books:-
Tour the Algarve, Portugal
Tour the Beja District, Portugal

ebooks only:-
Tour the Football Clubs in the English Premier League
English Football – Tour the Soccer Clubs in the Top 4 Leagues
Tour the United States of America

Thank you for reading this book.

P.D. Cain

www.ingramcontent.com/pod-product-compliance
Lightning Source LLC
Chambersburg PA
CBHW050815290526
45792CB00001B/131